LOOk Closer

Bugs

DK

LONDON, NEW YORK, MUNICH,
MELBOURNE, and DELHI

Text by Sue Malyan
Editor Fleur Star
Senior art editor Janet Allis
Publishing manager Susan Leonard
Managing art editor Clare Shedden
Jacket design Simon Oon
Picture researcher Sarah Mills
Production Luca Bazzoli
DTP Designer Almudena Díaz

First American Edition, 2005

Published in the United States by
DK Publishing, Inc., 375 Hudson Street,
New York, New York 10014

05 06 07 08 09   10 9 8 7 6 5 4 3 2 1

A Cataloging-in-Publication record for this book
is available from the Library of Congress.

ISBN 0-7566-1432-5

Color reproduction by Colourscan, Singapore
Printed and bound in China by Hung Hing

Discover more at
www.dk.com

Contents

Look for us. We will show you the size of every animal in this book.

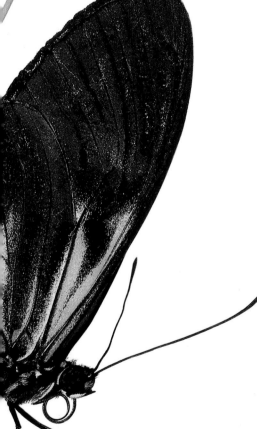

Spiked with poison

spiky

This postman caterpillar may be tiny, but it is heavily armed. Not only is it covered in sharp spines, but its body is full of poison.

sharp

I've got 12 eyes, but I can only see if it's light or dark.

prickly

This insect is so small it can disguise itself as bird droppings.

I won't always be a caterpillar. Soon I will change into a brightly colored butterfly.

nibble nibble

Did you know...

...The caterpillar can only use its first six legs for walking. Its other legs just have suckers for gripping.

Hopping along

This desert locust is still a young hopper. Its wings have not yet formed, so it moves around by hopping.

I like to be with other hoppers. The more of us there are, the faster we all hop!

These are my jaws. I use them like teeth to bite and grind up my food.

I make my chirping noise by rubbing my back legs against these hard veins on my wings.

chirp

chirp

chirp

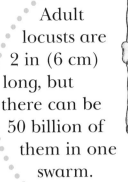

Adult locusts are 2 in (6 cm) long, but there can be 50 billion of them in one swarm.

Look how long and strong my back legs are! I can jump 10 times my own length.

Did you know...

... Locusts are grasshoppers that move in swarms. When a swarm eats, it can ruin whole crops.

Flying beetle

This cardinal beetle has been feeding on the pollen in a flower. When it is finished, it lifts its bright red wing cases, ready to fly off.

I can't fly very fast.

Did you know...

... Birds know that a brightly colored insect tastes nasty and could even be poisonous.

These are my antennae. I use them to feel and to smell.

When I'm flying, I lift up my wing cases out of the way of my wings.

Cardinal beetles are ½ in (1.4 cm) long, but they are easy to spot.

I've had my fill—I'm off.

Deadly sting

If you ever spot a scorpion, keep out of its way! The stinger on the end of its tail is so poisonous that it could kill you.

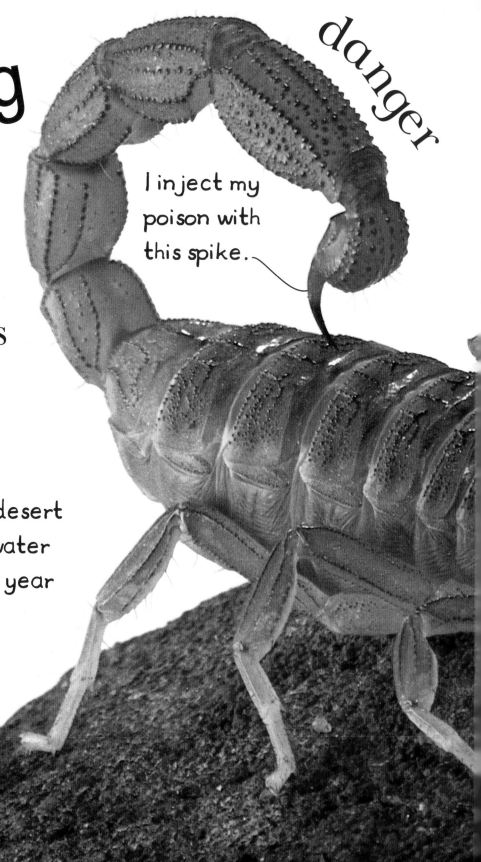

I inject my poison with this spike.

I can survive in the desert for months without water and for more than a year without food.

Scorpions are deadly but small— just 4 in (10 cm) long.

I've got four pairs of eyes on top of my head, but I can't see very well.

If I want a snack, I grab an insect or a lizard in my two pincers.

Boo!

Did you know...

... The scorpion's poison makes its victim unable to move. It would kill a person in a few hours.

Fast flier

This dragonfly is taking a rare break, resting on a plant. It spends hours in the air without landing.

My eyes are so big they cover most of my head.

I'm very good at spotting things that move around, like my dinner!

My spiky legs help me hang on to slippery surfaces.

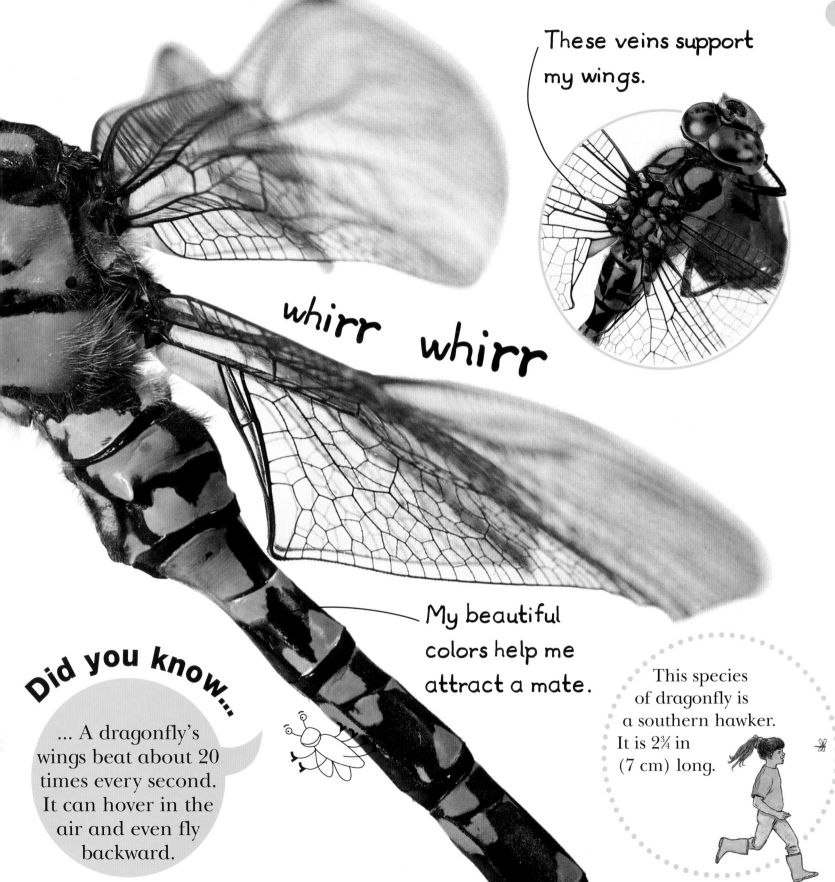

These veins support my wings.

whirr whirr

My beautiful colors help me attract a mate.

Did you know...

... A dragonfly's wings beat about 20 times every second. It can hover in the air and even fly backward.

This species of dragonfly is a southern hawker. It is 2¾ in (7 cm) long.

Watch me run

Scuttling over the hot desert rocks, this ground beetle is chasing a spider. It has long legs and can run really fast as it hunts its prey.

My skeleton grows on the outside of my body. It makes a hard, protective case.

twitch twitch

My jaws are outside my mouth. I use them to grab my prey and chop it up.

Did you know...

... If it is attacked, the ground beetle squirts its enemy with a liquid that burns.

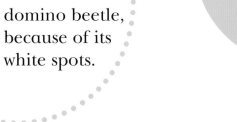

This kind of ground beetle is called a domino beetle, because of its white spots.

I can't fly because my wing cases are stuck together.

Where'd that spider go?

Babysitting bugs

When most insects lay eggs, they leave them alone. This female parent bug is different. She stays to guard her eggs and defend the young bugs against enemies.

We live on birch leaves because they are full of nice, juicy sap to drink.

Even fully grown parent bugs are just ¼ in (0.6–0.8 cm) long, so it's easy for lots of babies to fit onto one leaf.

These are my babies. They stay close so that I can protect them.

Flutter, flutter

With a flutter of red and black wings, a postman butterfly lands on a passion flower, looking for a drink of nectar.

flap

flutter

This butterfly has large wings for the size of its body. The wings can grow to 3 in (8 cm) across.

This curled-up tube is my proboscis. I use it like a straw to suck up my food.

My wings are covered with scales.

Did you know...

... Female postman butterflies lay up to 500 eggs, but only a few of them survive to be adults.

Mmm, passion flower—my favorite!

upside-down

My black and red colors show that I am poisonous. Birds soon learn to leave me alone.

Killer sucker

Dung flies are always on the lookout for animal poop, because that's where they lay their eggs.

My yellow "fur" shows that I'm a male. Females are gray.

buzz buzz buzzzzz

I've got a big mouth! It's great for sucking up liquid.

These tiny flies are less than ½ in (1 cm) long.